MY BOOK OF Amazing Achievements

Created By April Chloe Terrazas

My Book of Amazing Achievements. April Chloe Terrazas, BS University of Texas at Austin.
Copyright © 2013 Crazy Brainz, LLC

Visit us on the web! www.Crazy-Brainz.com

instructions:

Choose a different achievement each day
by folding the page over in the morning.

At the end of the day, bring the book to your teacher to be
signed. You can do each acheivement up to 5 times.

REMEMBER, you will only get a signature
if you achieve all day!

Show your teacher, your parents, and your friends
how AWESOME you are.
Get this book COMPLETELY SIGNED!!!

You can also use this book at home and
get your AMAZING ACHIEVEMENTS signed by your parents!

You are Great!

Happy Patrol

Smile at your classmates and be friendly to EVERYONE!

Date   Teacher Signature

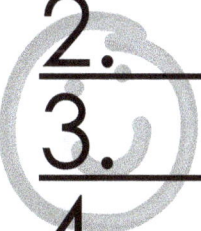

1. _____

2. _____

3. _____

4. _____

5. _____

Amazingly Neat

Keep your desk area neat and clean.

Date   Teacher Signature

1. _____

2. _____

3. _____

4. _____

5. _____

Recycling Leader

**Collect papers, cups
and other recyclable items.
Place them in the recycling bin.**

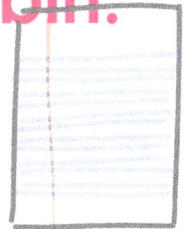

Date   Teacher Signature

1. _____

2. _____

3. _____

4. _____

5. _____

Leader of the Pack

Show you are a good leader by having a GREAT ATTITUDE wherever you are today.

Please

Have a nice day!

Thank You!

Date   Teacher Signature

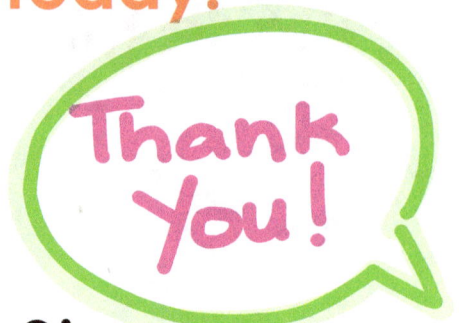

1. _____

2. _____

3. _____

4. _____

5. _____

Teacher Assistant

Be ready to help your teacher with any tasks for the day!

Date   Teacher Signature

1. _____

2. _____

3. _____

4. _____

5. _____

Awesome Helper

Help your teacher by passing out or collecting papers today.

Date   Teacher Signature

1. _____

2. _____

3. _____

4. _____

5. _____

Field Trip
BEST BEHAVED

You are the BEST behaved student on the field trip today. If you get this signed, you are REALLY AWESOME!

Date   Teacher Signature

1. _____

2. _____

3. _____

4. _____

5. _____

Wow!

Peer Assistant

Help your classmates if they do not know how to complete an assignment.

Date	Teacher Signature
1.	
2.	
3.	
4.	
5.	

Awesome Assignments

Complete ALL of your assignments today!

Date   Teacher Signature

1. _____
2. _____
3. _____
4. _____
5. _____

Lunch Leader

Show your classmates what AWESOME behavior looks like at lunch. Help your teacher pick up any missed trash or trays after lunch.

Date   Trash   Teacher Signature

1. _____

2. _____

3. _____

4. _____

5. _____

Line Leader

Shhh!

Stand up straight and walk quietly in the hallways.

Date   Teacher Signature

1. _____

2. _____

3. _____

4. _____

5. _____

Class Charmer

You are a GREAT teacher!

You did well!

Give complements to your classmates and your teacher.

Nice Work

Date   Teacher Signature

1. _____

2. _____

3. _____

4. _____

5. _____

Attentive Listener

Listen VERY carefully when your teacher is speaking to you or the class.

Quiet

Listen

Date   Teacher Signature

1. _____

2. _____

3. _____

4. _____

5. _____

Sneaky Walker

Walk quietly and quickly wherever your class goes today.

Great

Job!!!

Quick

Quiet

Date

Teacher Signature

1. _____

2. _____

3. _____

4. _____

5. _____

Sherlock Holmes

**If anyone needs help finding anything, YOU WILL HELP!
Assist your classmates and teacher if anything is missing or lost.**

Date   Teacher Signature

1. _____
2. _____
3. _____
4. _____
5. _____

Playground Coordinator

**Bring balls and toys to the playground and
BACK TO THE CLASSROOM.
You have a VERY important job!**

Date   Teacher Signature

1.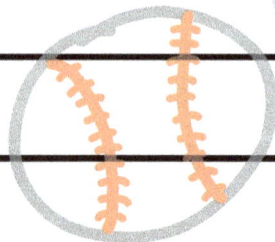
2.
3.
4.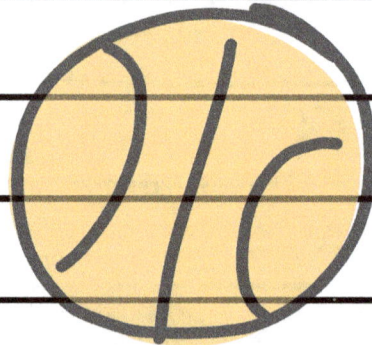
5.

Share the Love

Would you like to play with this toy?

Share with your classmates today.

Date   Teacher Signature

1. _____
2. _____
3. _____
4. _____
5. _____

Best Behaved

**This is a hard one to get!
You will <u>LISTEN</u> to your teacher,
<u>COMPLETE ASSIGNMENTS</u>,
<u>BE HAPPY</u> in class and
<u>HELP</u> when needed.**

AMAZING! *Way to go!*

Date   Teacher Signature

1. _____

2. _____

3. _____

Wow!

4. _____

5. _____

Amazing Handwriting

Your handwriting is going to be <u>VERY NEAT</u> today. Try to make it as neat as your teacher!

Amazing Handwriting!

Date   Teacher Signature

1. _____

2. _____

3. _____

4. _____

5. _____

Spill Patrol

Oops! **You are the person that your class needs to help clean up any spills.**

Date	Teacher Signature
1.	
2.	
3.	
4.	
5.	

Best Listener

You are an AMAZING listener!
Do not talk while someone else
is talking.

You're the BEST!

Date   Teacher Signature

1. _____

2. _____

3. _____

4. _____

5. _____

Calm and Quiet

Pay attention in class and complete assignments while being calm and quiet. If you have a question, __RAISE YOUR HAND__. Encourage your classmates to be calm and quiet too.

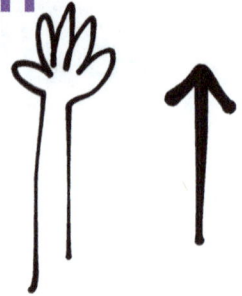

Date   Teacher Signature

1. _____
2. _____
3. _____
4. _____
5. _____

Best Reader

If you finish any
assignment today
before the class
is done, get
your favorite book
and read quietly.

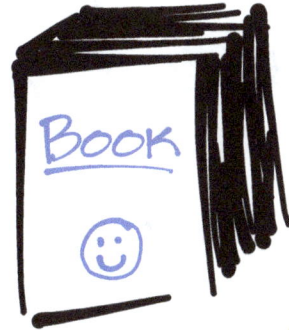

Book

:)

Date   Teacher Signature

1. _____

2. _____

3. _____

4. _____

5. _____

Task Master

**You will listen to your teacher and complete ALL assignments.
You are <u>SO AWESOME</u> because you will finish
all of your assignments today!**

Date   Teacher Signature

1. _____
2. _____
3. _____
4. _____
5. _____

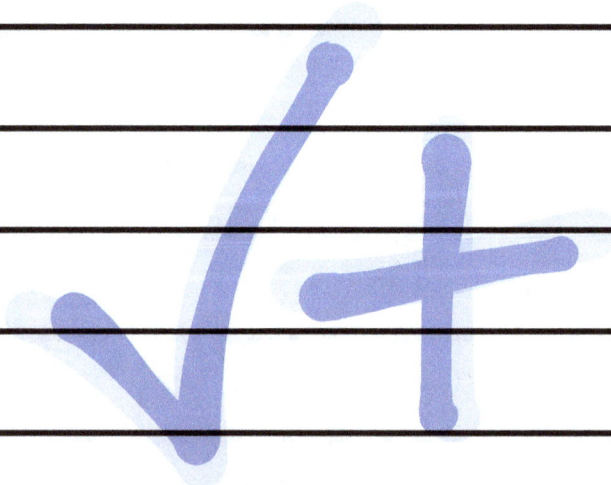

Playground Leader

Show your classmates what it looks like to be safe while playing on the playground.

Date   Teacher Signature

1. _____
2. _____
3. _____
4. _____
5. _____

Team Player

Work as a team with your classmates today. You may help push in chairs, clean up desk areas or assist the teacher. This is a VERY important job!

You Rock!

Date   Teacher Signature

1. _____

2. _____

3. _____

4. _____

5. _____

Intelli-KID

"Please pass the markers. Thank you very much."

You will speak clearly and intelligently. Your classmates will think you are in high school!

Date   Teacher Signature

1. _____
2. _____
3. _____
4. _____
5. _____

High-Fiver

When a classmate near you answers a question correctly, give them a high-five for being AWESOME.

Good Job!

	Date	Teacher Signature
1.		
2.		
3.		
4.		
5.		

Classroom Cleanup

You are VERY important because you will help clean up any messes in the classroom.

Date   Teacher Signature

1. _____

2. _____

3. _____

4. _____

5. _____

Happy Walker

You will walk quietly and with a smile!
NO RUNNING
unless you are on the playground.

Date   Teacher Signature

1. _____
2. _____
3. _____
4. _____
5. _____

SURPRISE!

You will surprise your teacher today with EXCELLENT behavior!

WELL DONE

Date   Teacher Signature

1. _____

2. _____

3. _____

4. _____

5. _____

Nicest Kid!

You are <u>VERY NICE to EVERYONE</u> you meet today. This includes your classmates and any other teachers or students at school.

Date   Teacher Signature

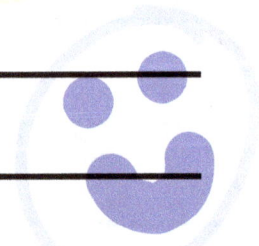

1. _____
2. _____
3. _____
4. _____
5. _____

Ready, Set, Go!

You are ready for any task today.
You get out your pencil or pen and
sit still, ready for the next assignment.
This is a GREAT achievement.

	Date	Teacher Signature
1.		
2.		
3.		
4.		
5.		

Best Listener

While anyone is speaking,
you remain quiet.
This is respectful and
your teacher will be proud of you!

Date   Teacher Signature

1. _____

2. _____

3. _____

4. _____

5. _____

Courteous Kid

Please

Thank You

Excuse Me

You can go first ☺

Being courteous is important. It means that you are polite, respectful and considerate.

Date   Teacher Signature

1. _____

2. _____

3. _____

4. _____

5. _____

Super Sitter

Stay in your seat unless your teacher tells you to get up. Encourage your classmates to follow your wonderful example.

Date   Teacher Signature

1. _____

2. _____

3. _____

4. _____

5. _____

Good Neighbor

Nice
Helpful
Respectful

Be nice, helpful and respectful to the students around you.

Date   Teacher Signature

1. _____

2. _____

3. _____

4. _____

5. _____

Kind Voice

Use a <u>kind and quiet voice</u> today.
Raise your hand to ask questions.
Do not interrupt the person speaking.

Date　　　　Teacher Signature

1. _____
2. _____
3. _____
4. _____
5. _____

Stay Busy!

If you complete an assignment before everyone is done, get out a book and read or draw quietly. Stay busy using your AMAZING brain until the teacher gives the next assignment.

Date   Teacher Signature

1.

2.

3.

4.

5.

READ! DRAW!

Follow the Rules!

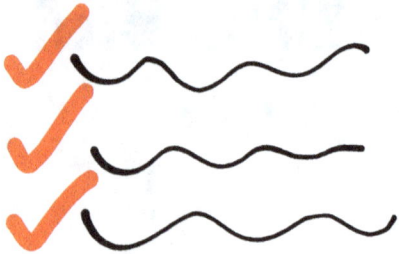

Be an AMAZING student and <u>follow all class rules</u> today! Your teacher and classmates will be very impressed.

RULES

Date   Teacher Signature

1. _____

2. _____

3. _____

4. _____

5. _____

You are an AMAZING Achiever!

Make up your own amazing acheivement here:

Date   Teacher Signature

1. _____

2. _____

3. _____

4. _____

5. _____

www.ingramcontent.com/pod-product-compliance
Lightning Source LLC
Chambersburg PA
CBHW080946050426
42337CB00056B/4857